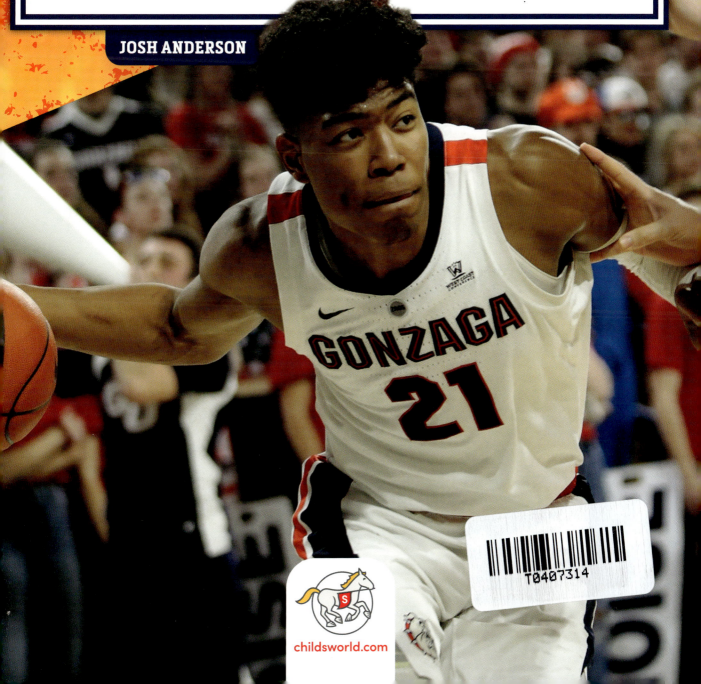

GONZAGA UNIVERSITY

JOSH ANDERSON

Published by The Child's World®
800-599-READ • www.childsworld.com

Copyright © 2024 by The Child's World®
All rights reserved. No part of this book may be reproduced or utilized in any form or by any means without written permission from the publisher.

Photography Credits
page 1: ©William Mancebo/Stringer/Getty Images; page 2: ©William Mancebo/Stringer/Getty Images; page 5: ©FPG/Staff/Getty Images; page 7: ©Stephen Dunn/Staff/Getty Images; page 8: ©Sean M. Haffey/Staff/Getty Images; page 9: ©William Mancebo/Contributor/Getty Images; page 11: ©Ethan Miller/Staff/Getty Images; page 12: ©Douglas Stringer/Icon Sportswire DIP / Newscom; page 15: ©Lance King/Contributor/Getty Images; page 16: ©Jamie Squire/Staff/Getty Images; page 17: ©William Mancebo / Contributor / Getty Images; page 18: ©Sooburn Im/Contributor/Getty Images; page 21: ©Focus On Sport/Contributor/Getty Images; page 23: ©James Snook/ZUMApress/Newscom; page 24: ©John Todd/Contributor/Getty Images; page 25: ©Jonathan Ferrey/Staff/Getty Images; page 27: ©Jamie Squire/Staff/Getty Images; page 28: ©Sooburn Im/Contributor/Getty Images; page 29: ©Lachlan Cunningham/Contributor/Getty Images

ISBN Information
9781503885196 (Reinforced Library Binding)
9781503885448 (Portable Document Format)
9781503886087 (Online Multi-user eBook)
9781503886728 (Electronic Publication)

LCCN 2023907973

Printed in the United States of America

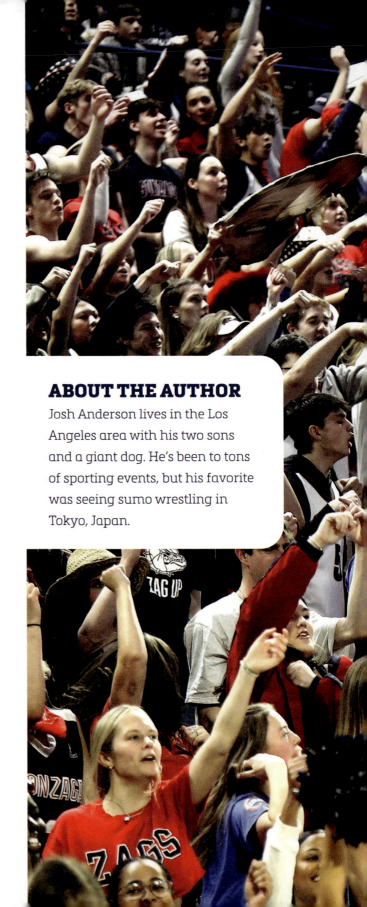

ABOUT THE AUTHOR

Josh Anderson lives in the Los Angeles area with his two sons and a giant dog. He's been to tons of sporting events, but his favorite was seeing sumo wrestling in Tokyo, Japan.

CONTENTS

CHAPTER ONE
Origins . . . 4

CHAPTER TWO
Rivalries . . . 10

CHAPTER THREE
Great Moments . . . 14

CHAPTER FOUR
All-Time Greats . . . 20

CHAPTER FIVE
The Modern Era . . . 26

Glossary . . . 30

Fun Facts . . . 31

One Stride Further . . . 31

Find Out More . . . 32

Index . . . 32

CHAPTER ONE

Origins

Gonzaga University started as Gonzaga College in 1887. The school is located in Spokane, Washington. Gonzaga was started by an Italian priest. He wanted to provide education to settlers in the Pacific Northwest of the United States. In 1912, the school became Gonzaga University. The school admitted women for the first time in 1948. When the school opened in 1887, there were only seven students. Today, around 7,000 people go to Gonzaga.

Men's basketball began at Gonzaga in the early 1900s. The team had its first game against another college in 1906. In 1921, the team officially became the Bulldogs. Gonzaga joined the **NCAA** in 1958. When the Big Sky **Conference** formed in 1963, Gonzaga was one of six teams in the new league. In 1979, the Bulldogs moved to the West Coast Athletic Conference. It later became the West Coast Conference (WCC). Gonzaga has played in the WCC ever since.

Gonzaga's men's basketball team does battle with the Oregon State Beavers in 1957.

Women's basketball existed at the school as early as 1960. But Gonzaga's women's team officially joined the NCAA in 1987. The women's team is also a part of the WCC.

Gonzaga's first men's basketball star was Frank Burgess, a six-foot-one (185.42 centimeters) guard. Burgess led the nation in scoring in 1960–61 when he averaged 32.4 points per game. The team had other star players over the years but did not make its first appearance in the **NCAA Tournament** until 1995.

Gonzaga University Bulldogs

TEAM NAME: Gonzaga Bulldogs

FIRST SEASON: 1906 (Men's Team); 1960 (Women's Team)

CONFERENCE: West Coast Conference (WCC)

CONFERENCE CHAMPIONSHIPS: 28 (Men's Team); 18 (Women's Team)

HOME ARENA: McCarthey Athletic Center

NCAA TOURNAMENT APPEARANCES: 25 (Men's Team); 14 (Women's Team)

NATIONAL CHAMPIONSHIPS: 0 (Men's Team); 0 (Women's Team)

Three Gonzaga defenders try to stop a Loyola Marymount player from taking a shot.

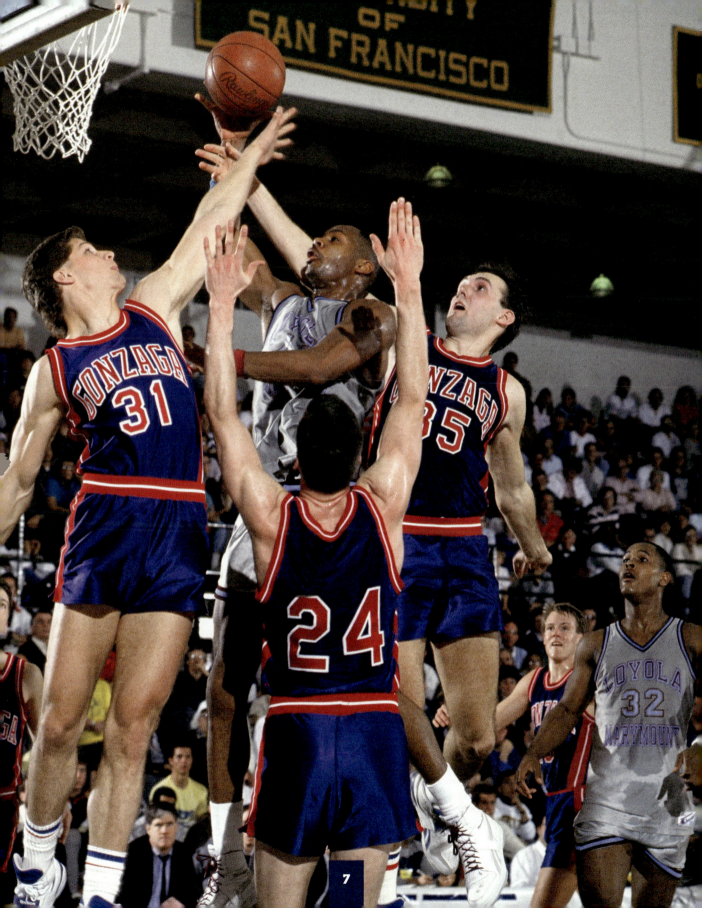

ORIGIN OF TEAM NAME

During the 1910s and 1920s, Gonzaga's teams were called the Blue and Whites or the Fighting Irish. In 1921, a reporter wrote that Gonzaga's players fought hard like bulldogs. The school adopted Bulldogs as the team name in all sports. Today, the school's mascot is called Spike the Bulldog. While all Gonzaga teams are called the Bulldogs, many fans also refer to the team as the Zags.

Guard Maria Stack was a star for the Gonzaga women's team during the program's early days. In 1984–85, she set a school record that stood for more than 25 years by scoring 707 points. That year, Stack was awarded with the Frances Pomeroy Naismith Award. This honor was given to the nation's best female basketball player under five-foot-eight (172.72 cm) between 1984 and 2014. The women's team first played in the NCAA Tournament in 2007.

Today, the men's and women's Bulldog teams are powerhouses in the WCC. Both teams won the conference most years during the 2000s. The women's team has **qualified** for 13 of the past 14 NCAA Tournaments. The men's team has played in every tournament since 1999.

Bulldogs guard Keani Albanez (right) drives to the basket during a 2015 NCAA Tournament game.

CHAPTER TWO

Rivalries

Gonzaga's main rival in men's basketball is fellow WCC school Saint Mary's College. Rivals are teams that have a long history of playing each other for the right to claim they are the best. Because the Bulldogs and the Saint Mary's Gaels play in the same conference, the teams meet at least twice every season. Since they are two of the best programs in the WCC, they often play a third time in the conference tournament.

Since the 2000-01 season, Gonzaga's men's team has won or tied for first place in the WCC conference every season except one. Saint Mary's won the crown in 2011-12 and tied with Gonzaga for the title three other times. The teams most recently tied for the title in 2022-23.

The Bulldogs have won 79 of their 112 games against the Gaels. But Saint Mary's has twice beaten Gonzaga when the Bulldogs were the number-one-**ranked** team in the country.

Gonzaga's Anton Watson (right) dunks during a rivalry game against the Saint Mary's Gaels.

Zags guard Jill Townsend was named Most Outstanding Player of the 2021 WCC Conference Tournament.

One memorable game between the teams was in the 2016 WCC Tournament final. The Gaels and Bulldogs tied for the regular season championship. Saint Mary's won both games during the regular season.

Gonzaga needed to beat St. Mary's. If they lost, they would break their NCAA Tournament appearance streak. Kyle Wiltjer scored 17 points and the Bulldogs beat their rivals 85–75.

Gonzaga's women's team has a longtime rivalry with Brigham Young University (BYU). Gonzaga has won just 2 of their 34 games against BYU, but they have often been first in the WCC ahead of their rivals.

In 2021, Gonzaga and BYU played in the final game of the WCC conference tournament. The winner would play in the NCAA Tournament. Both teams struggled to make shots. BYU held a 42–41 lead with under a second left in the game. Kaylynne Truong passed the ball to teammate Jill Townsend. Townsend had missed all five of her shots in the game so far. She caught the ball and immediately threw it up toward the basket. The ball swished through the hoop as the buzzer sounded. The Bulldogs were heading to the NCAA Tournament.

GONZAGA UNIVERSITY
VS.
BRIGHAM YOUNG UNIVERSITY

First Meeting:
2011 (Men's Teams); 1984 (Women's Teams)

Gonzaga's Record against BYU:
24–7 (Men's); 22–12 (Women's)

CHAPTER THREE

Great Moments

The 1999 Gonzaga men's team made the NCAA Tournament for only the second time in school history. The team was not yet the powerhouse of college hoops that they are today. The Zags were playing as a 10 **seed**. No one expected them to win any of their games in the tournament. But they managed to defeat the University of Minnesota in the first game. Then, they beat Stanford University in the second one. In the third game, the Bulldogs pulled off a one-point victory over the University of Florida to put them in the **Elite Eight**. The Zags were one win away from the first **Final Four** in school history.

Although Gonzaga's magical run in the 1999 NCAA Tournament ended in the next game with a loss to the University of Connecticut, the team has played in every NCAA Tournament since. The Zags finally made the Final Four for the first time in 2017. After beating the University of South Carolina in the national semifinals, they lost to the University of North Carolina in the championship game.

Zags guard Silas Melson (right) drives toward the hoop in the NCAA Tournament championship game against the North Carolina Tar Heels.

Jalen Suggs (center) sent Gonzaga to the 2021 National Championship Game with his last-second shot against the UCLA Bruins.

But the Zags were back in the Final Four just four years later. This time, Gonzaga entered the tournament ranked first in the country. They hadn't lost a game all year. They played a very close game against UCLA in the national semifinal that went to overtime tied 81–81.

With seconds left in overtime, the teams were still tied, 90–90. Gonzaga guard Jalen Suggs hit a three-pointer as the buzzer sounded to give the Zags a 93–90 victory. While their perfect season ended in the championship game with a loss to the Baylor Bears, 2020–21 was the greatest season in Bulldogs history so far.

The Gonzaga women's team made their greatest run in the NCAA Tournament in 2011. After defeating Iowa in the first game and UCLA in the second one, the Zags faced the Louisville Cardinals in the **Sweet 16**. The winner would play number-one seed Stanford in the Elite Eight.

After Gonzaga took a 35–24 lead at halftime, Louisville came back. The Cardinals got within three points with less than three minutes remaining.

THAT'S STRANGE!

The 2020 NCAA Tournament was canceled due to COVID-19. The COVID-19 **pandemic** shutdown affected businesses, sporting events, and entertainment around the world. Zags fans will always wonder what might have happened if that year's tournament had taken place. The Bulldogs finished the season 31–2 and were ranked second in the country. They had defeated successful teams such as Washington, Arizona, and North Carolina. Could 2020 have been the year the Zags finally won a national championship? No one will ever know.

Forward Melody Kempton was chosen for the 2021–22 All-WCC First Team.

Many of Gonzaga's points late in the game came from the free-throw line. The Bulldogs made 11 of their 12 free throws in the closing minutes. When the game ended, the Zags led 76–69. They had made the Elite Eight for the first time in school history. Even though they lost their next game, the season had been the team's best ever.

Another memorable victory for Gonzaga's women's team was their triumph over BYU in the 2022 WCC Tournament final. The Cougars were the 15th-ranked team in the country and the WCC regular season champions. Gonzaga's best chance at going to the NCAA Tournament was winning the tournament final. With 15 points from forward Melody Kempton, the Zags beat BYU 71–59 and earned another trip to the tournament.

CHAPTER FOUR

All-Time Greats

Point guard John Stockton was a star for Gonzaga long before the school ever played in the NCAA Tournament. He was a part of the team from 1980 until 1984. Stockton is Gonzaga's all-time leader in steals, with 262. He also ranks fifth all-time with 554 career **assists**. Stockton helped the Zags win games, but he also brought national attention to the university. He was the first WCC Player of the Year in school history. He was also the first Bulldog ever picked in the first round of the NBA **Draft**. Stockton went on to have a legendary NBA career. He's the NBA's all-time leader in assists, with 15,806.

Current men's basketball coach Mark Few holds the school record for coaching victories with 689. He ranks 26th all-time among all Division I men's coaches. Few became the head coach at Gonzaga in 2000. The Zags have never missed the NCAA Tournament with him in charge.

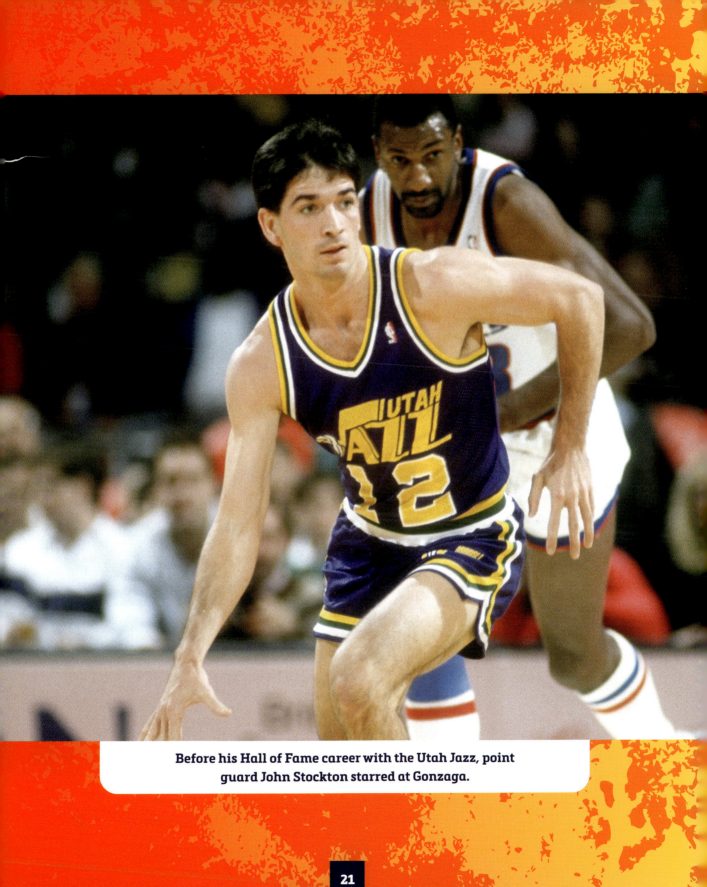

Before his Hall of Fame career with the Utah Jazz, point guard John Stockton starred at Gonzaga.

THE G.O.A.T.

Point guard Courtney Vandersloot played for Gonzaga from 2007 to 2011. She won the WCC's Player of the Year award three times while on the team. As a senior, Vandersloot set the NCAA's single-season assists record with 367. She ranks third all-time with 1,118 career assists. She is also the first Division I player, male or female, to reach 2,000 points and 1,000 assists. Vandersloot was picked third overall in the WNBA Draft. She played 11 seasons with the Chicago Sky and joined the New York Liberty in 2023. Vandersloot has led the league in assists six times during her pro career.

One of the top stars in Few's time as coach was Adam Morrison. Morrison played three seasons for the Zags from 2003 to 2006. Although he didn't play a full four years, he still ranks fourth in school history with 1,867 career points. Morrison was second in the nation in scoring in 2005–06 with 926 points and was named WCC Player of the Year. He was the third overall pick in the 2006 NBA Draft. He played four seasons in the NBA for the Charlotte Bobcats and the Los Angeles Lakers.

Heather Bowman was a forward for Gonzaga's women's team from 2006 to 2010. She helped lead the Bulldogs to the NCAA Tournament three times. Bowman scored 2,165 points in her career, which ranks first in school history and third in WCC conference history. She also ranks third in school history with 874 career rebounds. Bowman was the WCC's Player of the Year for the 2007–08 season.

Zags legend Courtney Vandersloot takes a shot in a WCC Tournament game.

Adam Morrison connected on almost 43 percent of his three-point shots during his last season with the Bulldogs.

In recent years, the Truong twins have starred for the Zags women's team. Kayleigh Truong was an All-WCC guard in 2021–22 when she averaged 11.2 points per game. Her twin sister Kaylynne was named the WCC's Player of the Year in 2022–23 after averaging 15.8 points and 5 assists as a senior. Kaylynne's 415 assists rank sixth in school history.

◀ All-WCC guard Kayleigh Truong shoots over her defender during the NCAA Tournament.

CHAPTER FIVE

The Modern Era

After winning the WCC regular season, the Gonzaga women's team finished 28–5 during the 2022–23 season. It was their seventh season playing in the NCAA Tournament under coach Lisa Fortier. The year came to a disappointing end when the Zags lost the first-round game 71–48 to Ole Miss. One of the team's stars in 2022–23 was WCC Player of the Year Kaylynne Truong. She paired up with forward Yvonne Ejim to lead the team that season. Ejim was chosen for the WCC's all-conference team after leading the Zags in scoring with 16.8 points per game.

The men's team won the West Coast Conference again in 2022–23. They finished with an overall record of 31–6. The Bulldogs advanced to the Elite Eight in the NCAA Tournament. They lost to the University of Connecticut, who went on to win the national title.

Forward Drew Timme led the Zags to three WCC conference titles and one shared conference title during his four years at Gonzaga.

Senior Drew Timme finished his memorable college career by averaging 21.2 points and 7.5 rebounds per game. The two-time WCC Player of the Year left Gonzaga as the school's all-time leading scorer with 2,307 points.

Both the men's and women's teams lost WCC Players of the Year after the 2022–23 season. Fans, players, and coaches all hope that the men's and women's teams will bring Gonzaga its first national basketball title in the near future.

TEARING UP THE LEAGUE!

Domantas Sabonis played for the Zags for two seasons from 2014 to 2016. As a sophomore, he averaged 17.6 points and 11.8 rebounds per game. After being drafted 11th overall in the 2016 NBA Draft, he became a star in the NBA. In 2023, Sabonis led the Sacramento Kings to their first **playoff** appearance since 2006. He also finished second in the NBA in **triple-doubles**.

◀ Twins Kayleigh (right) and Kaylynne Truong each played four seasons for the Zags from 2019 to 2023.

GLOSSARY

assist (uh-SIST) a pass that leads directly to a basket

conference (KON-fuhr-enss) a group of teams that compete and play against each other every season

draft (DRAFT) a yearly event when the best amateur players are picked by professional teams

Elite Eight (uh-LEET AYT) games between the top eight teams in the NCAA Tournament

Final Four (FY-null FOR) games between the top four teams in the NCAA Tournament

NCAA (National Collegiate Athletic Association) a group that oversees college sports in the United States

NCAA Tournament (TUR-nuh-ment) a competition between 68 teams at the end of the college basketball season that decides the national champion

pandemic (pan-DEM-ick) a disease that spreads across many countries and affects people around the world at the same time

playoff (PLAY-auf) a game after the end of a team's regular season

qualified (KWAL-uh-fyd) became eligible for a competition based on previous wins or performances

ranked (RANKT) placed on a list of individuals or teams that have accomplished high statistics in sports

seed (SEED) a team's ranking within a tournament

Sweet 16 (SWEET six-TEEN) games between the top 16 teams in the NCAA Tournament

triple-double (TRIH-puhl DUH-buhl) a game in which a player accumulates 10 or more in 3 statistical categories (example: points, rebounds, and assists)

FUN FACTS

- In addition to being the school's all-time leader in assists, point guard Josh Perkins, who played from 2015 to 2019, leads the men's team in games played, with 153.

- Amy Simpson set the Gonzaga women's single-game record with 38 points in a 1983 game against Lewis-Clarke State College.

- Casey Calvary played at Gonzaga from 1997 to 2001. He's the school's all-time leader in blocked shots, with 207.

- The Bulldog women had their highest-scoring game ever against Whitman College in 2011. They won the game 114–40.

- The Gonzaga women's team played the University of Oregon eight times between 1987 and 2004 but failed to win a single game against the Ducks.

ONE STRIDE FURTHER

- Gonzaga has been very successful on the court, but neither its men's nor women's team has ever won a national championship. How important is winning a title when judging the best teams of all time? Should Gonzaga be considered among the best? Or do they need to win a title first?

- Write a list of your favorite college basketball players. Include two things about each player that make them your favorite. Is it the way they play? Their attitude on the court? What else?

- Ask your friends and family members about their favorite sport. Keep track, and make a graph to see which sport wins.

FIND OUT MORE

IN THE LIBRARY

Berglund, Bruce. *Basketball GOATs: The Greatest Athletes of All Time.* New York, NY: Sports Illustrated Kids, 2022.

Buckley, Jr., James. *It's a Numbers Game! Basketball.* Washington, DC: National Geographic Kids, 2020.

Williamson, Ryan. *College Basketball Hot Streaks.* Parker, CO: The Child's World, 2020.

ON THE WEB

Visit our website for links about Gonzaga basketball:

childsworld.com/links

Note to Parents, Caregivers, Teachers, and Librarians: We routinely verify our web links to make sure they are safe and active sites. So encourage your readers to check them out!

INDEX

Bowman, Heather, 22
Burgess, Frank, 6
Ejim, Yvonne, 26
Few, Mark, 20, 22
Kempton, Melody, 19
Morrison, Adam, 22, 25
Sabonis, Domantas, 29
Saint Mary's College, 10, 12
Spokane, Washington, 4
Stack, Maria, 8
Stockton, John, 20–21
Suggs, Jalen, 16–17
Timme, Drew, 27, 29
Truong, Kayleigh, 25, 29
Truong, Kaylynne, 13, 25–26, 29
West Coast Conference (WCC), 4, 6, 8, 10, 12–13, 19–20, 22, 25–26, 29